Knowledge encyclopedia - Vivero

Hi, I'm Uncle Ken Jones. Today, we're going to learn about the amazing bottle-nosed dolphin. The dolphin is a sacred animal to our people. Whales and dolphins are called Kaantabul in Boandik culture. They live in our sea country. Our First Nations people have lived and worked with dolphins for thousands of years to herd and catch fish together.

2

3

You can find bottle-nosed dolphins living in the oceans off Australia's coast. They are called social animals. This means that they love to live and hunt in groups or pods. Some pods can be small. Some pods can have over one thousand dolphins. First Nations people worked with these pods to hunt fish.

Knowledge Books and Software

5

Knowledge Books and Software

The bottle-nosed dolphin gets its name from the shape of its snout. It looks like a short, round bottle. This helps the dolphin to hunt out shellfish. Dolphins feed on bigger fish like Tommy Ruff and salmon. They also love squid and cuttlefish. Their body is very smooth, and they can swim up to 35km/hour. This makes them fast hunters!

Knowledge Books and Software

7

Dolphins are warm-blooded animals. They give birth under water. Mum gently nudges her baby calf to the surface so it can take its first breath of air. The calves suckle from their Mum for nearly two years. They stay with her for about four years. They are then old enough to look after themselves.

Knowledge Books and Software

9

Dolphins are very smart animals. They use signals to find their fish and to find their way around. It works like this:

1. The dolphin makes a clicking sound.

2. This clicking sound bounces off things around them.

3. The sound bounces back to the dolphin.

4. This sound tells the dolphin how far away and how big something may be.

Knowledge Books and Software

Knowledge Books and Software

Dolphins work together in groups to herd and trap fish. They round them up and then dive into the middle of the school to catch their fish. First Nations people joined in the hunt in their bark canoes. They shared their catch with the dolphins.

Knowledge Books and Software

13

Dolphins love to play. They love surfing the waves. They can sometimes be seen sharing a wave with a surfer. If you are ever at sea, look out just below the front of the boat. You may see dolphins surfing the bow wave! Dolphins used to swim with our First Nations people as well. They would follow the canoes and help with the catch.

Knowledge Books and Software

15

Today, some people still call dolphins in close to shore to help catch fish. They do this by whistling and clapping underwater. The dolphins chase the fish into the shallows. The fish are then caught in nets. The fishermen will then share their catch with the dolphins.

Knowledge Books and Software

17

Dolphins need to watch out for white pointer (great white) sharks and orcas (killer whales). They also need to be careful of fishermen's guns and nets. Not all fishermen respect their environment. Their greed and careless actions can harm dolphins. These people need a lesson in Caring for Country!

Knowledge Books and Software

The other danger to dolphins is getting stuck on the sand. This is called stranding. Most of the time, their signals stop them from getting stranded. However, things around them can mix up their signals. They can find themselves in shallow water. Once dolphins are stuck on the beach, they are in a lot of trouble.

Knowledge Books and Software

Dolphins are a very important part of the food chain. They have been very important to our First Nations people for thousands of years. They are still a sacred animal to us today. Dolphins also bring people much joy. Let us all try hard to keep them safe and healthy for our future generations.

Knowledge Books and Software

23

Word bank

connection

whistling

bottle-nosed

orcas

dolphin

stranding

social

echoes

thousand

generations

cuttlefish

warm-blooded

mammals

suckle

environment

canoes

Knowledge Books and Software